footsteps
in the
garden

Bob MacKenzie

Acknowledgements

Versions of "among the hoodoos," "black rain," "edge," "jazz café," "rain," "read aloud," "the girl," "the woman," and "upstairs the dogs howl" have been published in *somewhere still in wind the tree is bending* (Silver Bow Publishing, 2018).

Versions of "edge," "I would photograph you," "some times of night," "the girl," and "The Train," have been published in *Agapé Heaven & Earth* (Dark Matter Press, 2015).

Versions of "edge," "the dark shimmering deep," and "the girl," have been published in *On Edge* (Dark Matter Press, 2012).

"black rain" has previously been published in the journal *Ottawa Poetry Magazine*, December 18, 2018.

"eden" has previously been published in the anthology *The Ultra Short Best Verse* (Beret Days Press, an imprint of The Ontario Poetry Society, 2013).

A version of "evening rain" has appeared in the journal *Rat's Ass Review*, Winter 2018.

"footsteps in the garden" has previously been published in the journal *Vallum: Contemporary Poetry*, Issue 16:2, September 2019.

"garden party" has previously been published in the journal *Picaroon Poetry*, Issue #12, May 20, 2018.

"Hands" has previously been published in *Origins*, First Issue, Fourth Volume, 1973.

"in the midst of things" has been published in Poetry and Covid, a project funded by the UK Arts and Humanities Research Council, University of Plymouth, and Nottingham Trent University, 2020.

"I would photograph you" has previously been published in the anthologies *Persian Sugar in English Tea: The Bilingual Anthology of Contemporary Love Poems* (Independent Publishing, 2018), *The Picture Perfect Poetry Chapbook Anthology* (Ontario Poetry Society, 2015), *BFW Bound: Instant Anthology*, limited edition (BookFest Windsor, 2012) and *That Not Forgotten* (Hidden Brook Press, 2011).

An earlier version of "jazz café" has previously been published as a letterpress broadsheet titled "Jazz One" (Thee Hellbox Press, 2017).

"New Worlds" has previously been published in *Legend*, Volume 2, Number 1, Winter 1973.

"Phoenix in the Garden" has previously been published in the Australian journal *Tweed*, Vol. 2, No. 3, March 1974 and the *Alberta Poetry Yearbook* (Canadian Author's Association Anthology, 1973).

"read aloud" has previously been published in the journal *Free Lit Magazine*, Volume 4, Issue 2, March 2018.

"recital" has previously been published in the anthology *Building Community: Select Stories and Poems from the 34th Annual NCWC* (CAA-NCR, 2021).

"snaps from the war" has previously been published in the journal *Rat's Ass Review*, Summer 2021.

"some times of night" has previously been published in The Tower Society anthology *Pine's the Canadian Tree* (1974) and in the journals *Janus & SCTH* (1973), and *The Tower* (1970).

"the dance" has previously been published in the journal *Bareback* (2013).

"the dark shimmering deep" has previously been published in the journal *Windsor Review*, Vol. 41. No. 1, Spring 2008.

"the obelisk" has previously been published in the journal *Terror House Magazine*, March 16, 2019.

"the soft side" has previously been published in *Free Lit Magazine*, Volume 5, Issue 2, March 2019.

"The Train" has previously been published in The Tower Society anthology *Pine's the Canadian Tree* (1974), and the journal *The Tower* (1973).

"the woman" has previously been published in the journal *Alien Pub Magazine*, April 13, 2018.

A version of "this love" has appeared in the journal *Rat's Ass Review*, Summer 2017.

"upstairs the dogs howl" has previously been published in the journal *Literary Review of Canada* (May, 2017).

I further acknowledge the the influence of and borrowings in "edge" from:

- Desiderata - Max Ehrmann
- Hollow Men (The) - Thomas Stearns Eliot
- Howl - Allen Ginsberg
- If I Had a Hammer - Pete Seeger & Lee Hays
- Love Song of J. Alfred Prufrock (The) - Thomas Stearns Eliot
- Rubayyat of Omar Khayyam (The) - Edward Fitzgerald (trans.)
- Second Coming (The) - William Butler Yeats
- Sound of Silence (The) - Paul Simon & Art Garfunkel
- Still Falls the Rain - Dame Edith Sitwell
- What Have They Done to the Rain? - Malvina Reynolds

Contents

an american dream

in battered stetson and old jeans
he recalls the time of legends
puts on his black leather jacket
like armour of a knight of old
who longs to go on one last quest
revs up his rust-tub of a Ford
reckless races toward memory
wild west legend that never was
seeks fame the only way he can
trapped in the new digital world

snaps from the war

a woman's tear falls quiet to the road
a young girl cries out and runs away
shots are fired then there is silence
a man weeps as he falls to his knees

guards guide a man to a windowless van
a woman who has no more tears falters
a girl lies unmoving held by a woman
a car and a van drive toward the city

black rain

though there's no way to confirm
they say this storm began
on the other side of the world
perhaps in Fukushima or Israel
spread rapidly
wrapping everything
everywhere in darkness

a squirrel has died
above the ceiling tiles
in the hallway
outside my office

there are hundreds
everywhere
huge black flies

for so long
the storm has not abated
I've lost track of the days
spent under these
black clouds of ash
and the heavy rain
they bring with them

the streets
have become rivers
only the most courageous
and the foolish
venture out

from the window
in my office
I see the bodies
in the streets
whenever the fire
rains from the sky

Some say it's a sign from some god
predicted by ancient prophets
punishment for all the evils
of mankind
others say it's our own fault
abusing the natural order
with our science

it all sounds the same to me

all I know is
for more days than I can calculate
I've not left this campus
crawling like a rat
through the tunnels
to other buildings
then back to my office
with what food and supplies
I can scrounge

there are others too
students and professors
and university staff
wandering the tunnels

I do my best to avoid them
in their eyes
there's a desperation
I believe will become
dangerous

best to play it safe

in the midst of things

in empty streets of locked doors
shuttered windows and the dead
bodies on flatbeds to be buried
visions of saved souls raised up
fears of the armies of armageddon
in our time where is the poetry

there are wolves on the streets
foxes roam the shores of the lake
and the man who attacked a woman
in a racially motivated incident
became ill and died a week later
in this dream where are the poets

a man says let us go then you and I
along half-deserted streets at dusk
alive with lies and metaphors
where fog becomes terrifying cats
and I can't follow a line through it
past singers busking in the shadows

a woodworker plays jazz on the porch
a deep black pool opens under me
and I dive in face down on the road
broken by the impact of this dream
among the falling darker shadows
from which I hear the angels sing

don't detective me with your smiles
in this time of sad souls and eyes
tellers of tales and erstwhile legends
the new normal conspiracy theory
sirens sing to us day and night
in this time of pandemic dreams

from my perch high above the city
I hear more sirens sing every day
echo of death walking the streets
hear waves smash on ancient rocks
smell the stench of the river styx
cower safely alone in this tower

red lights break the dark like rubies
blood perhaps not gemstones but fluid
life bleeds out everywhere imaginable
still the sirens sing night and day
come join us here on the waiting rocks
come swim with us in the river styx

I have seen no three-headed dog
no sensual young ladies singing
have not tied myself to the mast
don't believe in myths of sirens
watch fire trucks and ambulances
blurs of the real below my tower

birds still sing in my garden
flowers bloom and plants prosper
eden at the top of the world
squalor below distant as hell
you by me singing in the garden
sharing wine is paradise enough

oasis of the gods in the clouds
mine is the only rooftop garden
others have the haven of balconies
dropping in a line to the street
smells of fire and smoke rise to me
barbeque or brimstone I wonder

where are the poets
the truthspeakers
the folk singers
authors and artists
the new prophets
recording our era

where is the poetry
where the legends
where the heroes
where the ballads
where the memory
the future needs

a postcard from south america
mentions the tree of many lives
speaks of bringing in the sheaves
but there is no rejoicing
lives cut short as harvest wheat
young fruit picked before time

this is not caution but fear
danger hides around each corner
walks with the wind behind you
isn't seen until you are caught
and death comes in small doses
where can we walk that is safe

there's little talk of the light
always the dark fills our days
a shadow over all our thoughts
without passion or hope then what
the light fades with the future
where can we go that is safe

this is the time of prophesy
fire and water and wind storms rage
plague ravages every nation
there are wars and rumours of war
murder is the greatest sacrilege
relentless death stalks the earth

seek hope where you can find it
practice black arts if you wish
trust magic to carry us through
invite a friend over for wine
wear a mask like a harem girl
in all things be safe and well

oppenheimer feared the worst
the end of the world with a bang
the poet got it right of course
this is the way the world ends
cowers in the falling dark
with a never-ending whimper

in my perch high above the city
I hear the soft sigh of fear
mist climbs the tower like a cat
the silence of grey streets rises
in my garden a cold wind blows
whispers warnings of end times

this is the cruelest death
the silence of sunday morning
alone in this private eden
what god has brought this on
the streets below are dead
in my heart I have died too

am I real here in this garden
what is dream and what is not
birdsong has left the garden
apples are no longer tempting
the woman may have been a dream
a serpent has fled into darkness

music floats up from mists below
frail songs of sirens that wake me
fogbound buskers perhaps after all
saxophone softened by concrete walls
hollow echoes of a distant piper
a woman casting her spell in song

where are the poets
the truthspeakers
the folk singers
authors and artists
the new prophets
recording our era

where is the poetry
where the legends
where the heroes
where the ballads
where the memory
the future needs

my home and garden float on the mist
the tower fades away in dawn's glow
I expect arthur's knights may appear
ghosts out of the mist around me
the woman sings a song from below
life is but a dream sh-boom sh-boom

mist sets damp on the flowers
on me in my garden alone
still her song pulls me away
her voice soft as morning mist
join me here on the waiting rocks
swim with me in the river styx

it's different inside the house
woken from a never-ending dream
world without end beyond this door
indoor echoes of a past life
home has become a fragile thing
I cling for fear of falling off

matryoshka worlds within worlds
this dollhouse at the centre
each room just like the others
each room empty even when full
empty worlds fade as night falls
a vision seen through the mist

how long since the stream dried up
windows on the world gone blank
watchful eyes closed or blinded
the system is down and out
radio silence and dead air
even indoors I taste the death

I am the master of the mists
sitting on top of the world
a small oasis in the clouds
unlike the statue in the desert
I am not yet crumbled and gone
my world vanished in the mist

there are rabbits on the lawns
coons roam the streets night and day
bats and rats and alley cats
wild things are taking the city
I see them whenever the mist clears
in all this where's the poetry

the sun shines down the tower
one vacant balcony to the next
ladder to the streets far below
my domain a world without life
wild things and the dead on flatbeds
in this dream where are the poets

going to hell is a practical thing
the elevator no longer works
our electric went down long ago
there's rubble in the stairways
this tower is a wretched wasteland
the only way down is to jump

through this mist I don't see the sun
yet the light seeps through the net
sunlight is trapped in rooftop panels
the tower has gone dark without power
rising above the dark streets below
home a shining beacon in the sky

where are the poets
the truthspeakers
the folk singers
authors and artists
the new prophets
recording our era

where is the poetry
where the legends
where the heroes
where the ballads
where the memory
the future needs

looking at the dark streets below
I am god up here in my small heaven
above I see only black nothing
am a speck waiting some rough beast
slouching down this infinite well
across my garden as shadows fall

what shall be left for me I wonder
when the gatherer comes to my door
shall he carry cross or sickle
shall he come in black or white
will he take me down the elevator
will I rise in passion skyward

we dig and find ancient cultures
famed for their beauty and wisdom
what will the future find of us
death perhaps and erased peoples
even pompeii's streets bore life
in the end what will we have left

my worst fears are imagined
a movement not seen but sensed
a footfall or a creaking door
threatening voices on the wind
danger hiding in the shadows
mine has become a shadow world

I walk through my garden alone
an uneasy wind whispers threats
shadows follow along the walls
who walks with me in the garden
the elevator no longer works
the only way out is down

I stand just at the edge of light
night's ink fills the city streets
stars are set in a dark blue sky
so long now since I've seen stars
hid always by never-ending mist
behind me the shadows remain

dawn comes over me slow and soft
mist curtains the sky once again
shades of night skulk in corners
there is a sense of butterflies
thoughts of birdsong left unheard
a life lived and lost so long ago

the song says life is but a dream
if this is a dream shall I wake
will the world be as before
will there be butterflies and birds
will there be no shadows following
it comes down to what is real

I loved a girl a long time ago
in fields of summer glory
walked hand in hand side by side
shared dreams through starlit nights
'til the shadows brought her death
end of our dream end of my life

long forgotten in the mist
precious memories come to me
woman I loved too long ago
home and children in the city
a peaceful cabin in the woods
I hear myself say fade to black

praise to the poets
the truthspeakers
the folk singers
authors and artists
the new prophets
recording our era

this is the poetry
these the legends
these the ballads
these the stories
this is the memory
the future needs

a canoe along the lakeshore
she waves from the cabin dock
boy and girl wade in the water
feels good to be coming home
memory fades into the mist
in my hand I feel the paddle

there's floods in the streets below
on sidewalks otters play games
in deep waters large carp swim
beavers gather debris for lodges
somewhere I hear a woman singing
on this tower there's only rain

the siren song calls me home
falling rain deepens the mist
even my garden is growing dark
shadows patrol garden paths
images from a past fade away
will this dark rain never stop

the man says let us go then
along half-deserted streets
alive with lies and metaphors
where fog becomes terrifying
and I can't find my way through it
though I hear the sirens singing

how I long for all this to end
to follow a song into the mist
the welcoming arms of the dark
a home outside this nightmare
world of fears and shadows
to sleep perhaps forever

sleep comes to me like drowning
drawn into deeper waters
the song of the woman calling
meet me where the ferry waits
come swim with me in the river
she draws me under and I drown

a current soothes and carries me
beyond dark waters of nightmare
into the river lethe and sleep
adrift between time and memory
the song again raising me up
from the dark into the light

the soft scent of warm earth
a chorus of birds singing
morning and the sun shining
warmth on my eyes waking me
where I slept under a tree
not a dark cloud overhead

a field of summer glory
wildflowers in the sunshine
prairie grasses and blue sky
a girl I love from long ago
walking slowly toward me
and I walk then run to her

they say life is like a dream
we meet in slow motion like that
she holds me close and I hold her
without talk we share our thoughts
of home and life with each other
walk hand in hand into the mist

praise to the poets
the truthspeakers
the folk singers
authors and artists
the new prophets
recording our era

this is the poetry
these the legends
these the ballads
these the stories
this is the memory
the future needs

New Worlds

What new worlds are hidden in your eyes?
I Magellan, who seek you in my circuit,
I love you,
I love you so!

My islands
Shine in your eyes.
'Round the world I have sailed upon their waters:
In their fire I have found eternal beachhead.
Brave new world,
I love you so!

I wonder what spear waits me on these shores
Oh hear the drumming wind.

Magellan, I shall claim this beach of yours
For you are my Cebu.

Raise my standard over your mountains;
place my body deep within your hills;
Magellan,
I come to you.

Phoenix in the Garden

Phoenix in the garden with an apple,
Water glass, Pandora's box, and wind,
Burn me in your flame and I will burn you,
Candle in the night, aflame, aflame!
I have held your heart in forest dapple,
Watching flames devour the golden find;
Icarus was no such moth as turns to
summer fire to burn and so to maim!
Phoenix, am I Icarus, so entwined,
Burning and plummetting now, urn to
Bear your ashes and wait more of the same
After festive times when I have dined,
Eaten Phoenix in the garden, learned to
Enter in the forest's golden game?

The Train

I have gone to the forest; you are sleeping in the town:
The fire is there in your town; I see, but I have water–
Shall I run the way, or become as the trees in the forest
Watching unquenchable you until the last spark dies,
And I take the train to town, and you ride to the forest–
Destination Eden, We come together, Love!

Now I am water wide; the land is your domain,
And I am cloud but not sky; the sky is yours alone.
Shall I rain and be yours? Or, rise to your blue bosom?
I ride your belt-line around, shuttlecock like Nancy,
Riding the train to town as your eyes come closer–
Destination Eden, We come together, Love!

love come soft

like morning mist over a mountain lake
or soft spring showers on a sunny day
my love came to me softly as the dawn
found and held my heart with her tender touch

it seems I have known my love for ages
longed for her from a distance in past lives
or have held her in my arms and loved her
until this woman entered all my dreams

this is not the hot passion of youth
hearts afire burning with primal desire
but a love new and surprising to me
as our hearts share this unexpected love

if this love in this life should ever end
it shall be held forever in my heart

edge

I've been standing in the cold falling rain
hearing the pulse of its heart beat down
seeing the dark images in its shadows
like the visions of ancient prophets
and I have seen that I stand in the gutter
between the edges between worlds apart
between gay and straight between rich and poor
between capital and commune between woman and man
between every possible polarity you can dream
looking at those edges not from the other side
but from somewhere between which is nowhere
and I have disappeared

don't get me wrong and don't get it twisted
it may after all have been only a dream
it may be I have seen nothing at all
and there was nothing at all to see in the rain
nothing but a magic shadow-show played in a box
lit by sun and moon against silhouettes of rain
around which we phantom figures come and go
the rain falling like knives slicing the dark
to create worlds then wash them away in a flash
lit by lightning that wakes me with a start

the words of the prophets echo down the centuries
truth grown tired and worn until the words are only dust
choking off the little breath we gasp to survive
the uncertain future we have created for ourselves
and in the words we hear echoing somewhere distant
the pulsing of a heartbeat pounding like a hammer
and feel that pulse drawing us out toward the edge

I've lived too long too near the edge
stood too close to where it happens
seen what I should not have seen
and heard it all and hear it still
in living dreams I cannot escape

there are people living on the edge
it is true, I have seen them there
clinging to the thin line between them
and the other side of their reality
have stood behind them as they clung
hopeless noses pressed to some window
to some place they could not enter
and I have stayed in the shadows
knowing they would not see me there

I have seen
I have seen
I have seen the best minds of my generation
and they are the same as those seen long ago
and they are not just America
and they are not destroyed after all
nor drag themselves through black streets
but stand waiting arm in arm to hold firm
against that rough beast, its hour come round
as it slouches unrelenting through every street
seeking some holy land and preordained birth

don't get me wrong and don't get it twisted
many people strive for high ideals
and everywhere life is full of heroism
but what does it matter in the end
what does it matter who is hero and who not

when it may after all be only a dream
and there was nothing at all to see but the rain
through which we come and go like phantoms
as the rain falls like knives slicing the dark
impulse of winter midnight streetlight rain
creating worlds that wash away in a flash
of lightning that wakes us with a start

there are people
cries in the wilderness
there are people
cries in the wilderness
there are people gathered in the streets
flooding the streets of every town and city
cries in the wilderness of grey streets
gathered with pens and with pitchforks
crying for justice all over this land
men and women standing arm in arm everywhere
warning of danger, crying out a warning
cries in the wilderness

in the room the people come and go
talking of what they have seen out there
but they don't go out there and they
and they don't do anything to stop it
in the dark in the room the people watch
in the silence in the room they listen
and drown awash in flickering images
and drown in the battle's sound and fury
across the universe and back again
and still falls the rain like helpless tears

he stands in the shadows of the evening rain
the gentle rain that falls for years
just a little boy standing in the rain
and rain keeps falling like helpless tears
still falls the rain with a sound like the pulse
the pulse of the heart that is changed to the hammer-beat
and rain keeps falling like helpless tears
the boy disappears

still I feel the heartbeat beating underneath every thing
the pulse of the heart that is changed to the hammer-beat
the pulse of the heart that hammers out love
the pulse of the heart that hammers out danger
the pulse of the heart that hammers out a warning
the pulse of the heart that hammers out hatred
while the rain keeps falling like helpless tears
while the best among us lose all conviction
while the worst grow full of passionate intensity
and the heartbeat pulses between every thing

don't get me wrong and don't get it twisted
it may after all have been only a dream
it may be I have seen nothing at all
and there was nothing at all to see in the rain
nothing but a magic shadow-show played in a box
lit by sun and moon against silhouettes of rain
around which we phantom figures come and go
the rain falling like knives slicing the dark
to create worlds then wash them away in a flash
lit by lightning that wakes me with a start

I've lived too long too near the edge
stood too close to where it happens
seen what I should not have seen
and heard it all and hear it still
in living dreams I cannot escape

the words of the prophets echo down the centuries
truth grown tired and worn until the words are only dust
choking off the little breath we gasp to survive
the uncertain future we have created for ourselves
and in the words we hear echoing somewhere distant
the pulsing of a heartbeat pounding like a hammer
and feel that pulse drawing us out toward the edge

surely some revelation is at hand
cries in the wilderness between the lines
this is the way the world ends
cries in the wilderness between the lines
this is the way the world ends
cries in the wilderness between the lines
this is the way the world ends
as we stand waiting arm in arm to hold firm
against that rough beast, its hour come round
as it slouches unrelenting through every street
seeking some holy land and preordained birth
and some ancient anarchy is loosed upon the world

but don't distress yourself with dark imaginings
no doubt the universe is unfolding as it should
and the dark you see is only rain falling

too long living not on the edge like some
too long living in the gutter flows
between the edges where the shadows flow
between the edges able to see the dark
see the dark that consumes their lives

I'm with you in Rockland he shouts out loud
cries from the wilderness with conviction
is anybody out there does anybody hear him
is Rockland just another dream in the dark
his voice an echo of something that is no more
a cry in the wilderness between the lines
I'm with you in Rockland fades in the distance
his voice disappears

but don't get me wrong and don't get it twisted
it may after all have been only a dream
it may be that I have seen nothing at all
and there was nothing at all to see in the rain
and I have disappeared

The Dark Shimmering Deep
for all the prophets in rags

I walk a wilderness of concrete streets,
I speak to the wind, I cry out to the sky,
and if heard at all I am never heeded.

I have seen how thin is the line and how frail
the membrane between us, between the light and
the dark shimmering entity ripping the membrane.

I have gone too far and have seen too much,
have stepped into that too near night and
seen the dark shimmering deep at its heart.

I have been to the heart of that place,
have been taken into its enchanted arms
and am not yet free nor ever will be.

I stand at the gate to that glorious garden,
barred by crested iron from going farther
into the light flooding its farthest reach.

I stand at the gate to a garden of darkness
as it draws me back, cling to the iron gate
between me and the sunlit garden just beyond.

I walk the streets of the city crying out
a warning; I stand before the masses moving
toward the dark beyond the swelling membrane.

I speak to the wind, I cry out to the sky,
and if heard at all I am never heeded;
I walk a wilderness of concrete streets.

I do not know who is walking beside me
and I do not hear the voice so near to me;
I am blinded and do not know this garden.

I think I walk through the garden alone,
but it seems that someone walks with me
and it seems that someone talks with me.

I have not walked at all in this garden
or that; a prophet in the wilderness
I stand between two worlds and cry out.

I feel in my hands the cold of iron bars
and my eyes burn with the light beyond
as the darkness pulls my heart and soul.

I walk the streets of the city crying out
a warning; yet still the masses swell and press
endless into that dark shimmering deep night.

I am invisible; I am unheard; I am a prophet
crying out in the wilderness; I am nothing
to those who seek the light through darkness.

It is done; I cling to this great iron gate
as worlds fall away from me, as worlds fall
and crash into chaos and darkness, and I cry.

I cry out to the sky, I speak to the wind,
I walk a wilderness of concrete streets,
and if heard at all I am never heeded.

shadow show

voices come and go as though passing
people talking perhaps but not words
echoes along a hall beyond these walls
lost in the depth of concrete and steel
cold as the dark of this damp prison
delusion in which I've become trapped

four lines made then crossed over
scratched tally covers these walls
top to bottom and end to end endless
calculations of eternity I think
wonder whose marks if not my own
count days and years in the dark

the window high above lets in day
light I feel not see on eyelids
closed against morning's burning
reminder of a lifetime in light
lost in a remembered reality
I wonder is this one a nightmare

my eyes open slow and careful
returning sight in half-light
deep blue dark as ink as night
dumpster in some alley by me
drums pound my temples as I sit
wake in the grit of this lane

it all goes black as eyes close
I pass fingers over the tallies
feel the rough marks on the wall
blue comes to mind a song perhaps
a wall of blue lost in memory
footsteps coming as drums beat

in a clear blue sky clouds glow soft
sunshine sparks off new winter snow
the air so crisp you could break it
twin lines curve toward infinity
like crumbs hoofmarks show the way
drawn on the field by a lone horse

I hear the lonesome steam whistle
feel more than hear the low rumble
the field slides away like a dream
sleep comes easy lulled by wheels
clickety-clack against steel rails
somewhere the sound of sleigh bells

this silence is worse than the guns
this waiting knowing they'll come
crouch and listen in deathly quiet
did a twig snap under some boot
rotors overhead break the silence
breathe now as long as you're able

blank white walls wait for writing
yet the moving finger has moved on
writ on other walls at other times
others read the writing on the wall
these bare white walls unsettling
guests held in Heaven's waiting room

this borrowed bed is not easy on me
I'll breathe as long as I'm able
the room is a barely furnished cell
locked at night they say for my own
protection from what or from whom
why has this white room no window

this place flashes into my memory yet
I may not ever have been in a prison
castle keep or dungeon torture chamber
gulag or guantanamo or death camp
memory a thousand-piece puzzle
hundreds of strategic pieces missing

I remember green fields and forests
city streets and shopping centres
somewhere a small house and family
behind the camera me or somebody
shooting small children on the lawn
shooting in the streets and running

down the long hallway boots march
missing pieces holes in my memory
dead-end alley with nowhere to run
children run and play on the grass
mother near the camera whispers
thank you darling I do love you

in a broken thousand-dream puzzle
which dream is real and which not
children play on suburban lawns
bullets and bombs and dead kids
city squares and villages bleed
missing pieces fall from drones

this six by eight box feels real
stainless steel bed and fixtures
real yet where are all the rats
where the voice behind the wall
seeking a friend and conversation
looking for a few missing pieces

projected by a spinning silver ball
light's rainbow whirls over dancers
pairs clinging through a slow waltz
song psychedelic as a dervish spell
slow-motion swirl across the floor
words float magic above the din

down by the bar seems more normal
one whiskey then get up and leave
roiling sound and colour hold me
one more whiskey then a last one
out of the haze she glides to me
angel gowned in flowing gossamer

whiskey or flickering strobe light
the walls close in and I am back
scratching tallies on grey concrete
an angel stands at the bar beside me
touches my arm and asks what's wrong
she says I'm Julia what's your name

I wake slowly to Julia's warmth
hold her close to me as she sleeps
rolls into me as though we are one
smiles slightly and starts to wake
eyes opening as she whispers soft
good morning sweetheart I love you

bathed in dawn's first golden glow
Julia and I walk along the beach
share the moment hand in hand
know that our love will endure
over the sea storm clouds darken
do I hear rain or marching feet

under a soft blue sky overcast by mist
two horses glide the cutter easily
set against a pristine white prairie
a few snowflakes sparkle as they fall
the magic of fairy lights in the air
the dapple greys whinny and carry on

the sun diffused by the mist softens
the scene the sleigh and its passengers
cross in near silence broken by a bird
heard in the sleigh by the girl and boy
four and five years old in fond memory
kept warm under that heavy buffalo robe

why can't I remember the man up front
his soft commands guiding the horses
two beautiful horses I remember well
and that pretty sleigh's curved dash
slow motion dashing through the snow
my sister and me caught in a dream

in this grey light I sense dawn coming
falling from the window high above me
no buffalo robe to comfort me as I wake
no sleigh gliding across the prairie snow
only the writing on the wall beside me
not words but cuts to count the years

the harsh voice of a crow calls to me
breaks through the waning dark of night
silence is broken in an instant falls
broken glass flutters to stone floors
quiet as snow falls in a winter prairie
a girl and boy ride across in a cutter

the man comes into my room every night
tells me I must be quiet and I forget
what happens that night or any other
even in this cell where shadows live
and I tell myself the man won't come
I feel him close to me and I'm afraid

where did that word cell come from now
a word I haven't called this place before
however long I've been among these shadows
unsure how long or what I did say or not
why have I only dreams and never memories
except of the man who comes into my room

I suppose that this room is a cell
barren but for a basic bed and toilet
washbasin and writing table with chair
no mirror so I forget even how I look
my room where I wait each night for him
one more shadow lurking and watching

night and day are hard to tell apart
uneasy sleep comes on a whim of light
as sudden waking is only a dream away
a lifetime it seems passing my eyes
more real than anything this can be
haunted by shadows lying in wait

footsteps in the night stop at my door
breathless I lie very still and wait
quiet as a lamb led to the slaughter
quiet as a young boy I may have been
terrified by the monster in my bed
still with me in my heart and soul

the soft effect of a light mist
thoughts of other early mornings
a dirt road out to the horizon
the red dog running ahead of me
ruddy flash among prime colours
the palette of this breaking day

set against a flawless blue sky
the muted sun hangs at the centre
framed by a cotillion of clouds
ahead of me the vanishing point
rich green of forest to my right
opposite grass and scrub meadows

I have been to this place before
more déjà vu than time remembered
the setter raises dust up ahead
and I hear the steam whistle wail
as in the distance a train rumbles
breaks the day's flawless silence

do I imagine the sound of drums
boots pounding across some square
running feet and gunshots echoed
or hear only a long freight train
fading past the vanishing point
then the quiet of a country road

in a meadow two deer look up at me
return to grazing in the long grass
as though to say he'll soon be gone
the dog stops on the road and waits
from somewhere far above the trees
the harsh voice of a crow calls me

a crow flies too high to be heard
above the flow of city streets
workers and shoppers throng beside
a rainbow river of cars and trucks
nowhere to go I follow the flow
between tall glass and concrete

I make my bike sound like a motorcycle
clothespin and cardboard between spokes
whir of the wheel and wind in my face
race with my friend down a country road
scrape of braked wheels on the gravel
the car is stopped and my friend gone

wraiths are filling the corners again
living shadows come into this space
I feel dark descend and fill the room
a man's footsteps almost at the door
in my bed I pull the blankets higher
there is heavy breathing next to me

in my darkness it is not enough
that I feel the pulse of the city
breathe the breath of the countryside
enjoy the sun's light and warm glow
not enough to fill this black hole
vacancy that sucks away my life

outside the door to the rooftop
wind harder than at street level
jacket zipped I walk to the edge
step onto the narrow wall there
look down from the tenth storey
prepared to fly away from it all

the voice behind me says step back
balanced on the edge I feel wind
gentle as that voice coaxing me
the wind says step ahead and fly
her voice behind me says come to me
cold sweat wakes me back in my bed

these autumn evenings are ideal
friends with guitars and folk songs
the fire dancing down by the lake
a lovely tableau or old painting
full moon on the water like a dream
darker night warns us of the fall

this deep black night becomes a void
discloses nothing but its own dark
shadow rises up these concrete walls
a furtive shibboleth I can't solve
all sight and all sound erased
in the dark of my bed I disappear

in the sandbox small armies march
fight wars manoeuver win and lose
nobody ever dies in sandbox wars
six year olds have immortal armies
out here we may not live forever
the smell of death is everywhere

we waltz round and round the floor
become as one while the band plays on
two souls in love's sublime harmony
beyond time's constraint for a while
lights dim and the music fades away
in the distance I hear a crow call

the warmth of her is a surprise
though it feels right to be naked
as I slowly wake into her soft back
left arm flung carelessly across her
heartbeat and breast under my hand
a shadow passes over and I shiver

not yet quite awake she rolls tight
against me as though we are one
joined in this dream for all time
words form in the air just past me
good morning sweetheart I love you
she slips back to sleep just for now

early sunbeams slip past the drapes
slant rays where motes of dust dance
starlike over to where we lie still
Julia and me here in our pure love
she asleep and I only just awake
troubled by the shadows of a dream

I hear drums beating or perhaps feet
marching along some parade ground
or down some long hallway toward me
I shiver and the shadow passes over
slant sunshine seeking to wake us
Julia leans into me with a soft moan

hand in hand we walk through sunlit fields
toward the forest paths we both love so
lovers sharing a sublime day together
a scene from a romantic movie I think
there's no sound as Julia turns slightly
on her lips the words I do love you

on the edge of this steel bench bed
elbows on knees and head in hands
my eyes closed to deny this space
any sense that what's here is real
feeling the floor as it rises up
I drown in this absolute darkness

I feel her soft against my back
roll over and watch her sleeping
wonder what this angel sees in me
in her sleep she smiles slightly
turns over to face away from me
the mist around us grows thicker

I wake slowly on this hard surface
the harsh voice of a crow calling
near the small window far above
gentle sunlight opens my eyes
the bed's stainless steel glowers
against the grey of these walls

marked only by scratched tallies
time here has no beginning or end
lines added day by day to the wall
how many days have I fallen down
beside the toilet or from the bed
how many more times must I fall

guns and machetes bring victory
the flow from murdered villages
blood turns river waters to wine
in the jungles death walks proud
I wake quickly in the black night
shiver in the cold of this cell

my father's war seems long ago now
falling bombs in the blitz whistled
spread terror just before they hit
weapon in hand I stand by a wall
see families in the street running
silent death destroys the hospital

weapon in hand I stand by this wall
held by something greater than fear
people running everywhere screaming
unsure when the next bomb will fall
on the street running unsure where
no whistle can make a difference

at dawn the silence of a marsh
one crow caws as the sun rises
a peeper frog calls to others
the choir of frogs fills the air
on a bullrush a redwing blackbird
seems to ask me why I have come

sometimes I see the wall's concrete
dissolve to mist across morning
marshland or the woods I walk
prairie grasslands blown gently
a soft bed in another room
where I wait for her to come

the flat of my hand on the wall
push as though to reach beyond
the wall only a dream or figment
I imagine but the concrete holds
once more I scratch a diagonal
line across four others waiting

borrowed voice of a sleeping crow
something calls black against black
through deepest night the dark cry
cuts into my dream without mercy
I wrap myself against the darkness
reaching through the window above

in time sleep comes again to me
curled in a ball on a cruel bed
whispers everything is alright
whisks me away to another world
where I forget which is dream
until I wake to the crow's call

morning bright through the window
one more scratch in the concrete
hope signified for another day
silence broken by the crow
ever closer sound of marching
is this the dream or perdition

visions come to me that seem real
peaceful walks on forest trails
a long beach of near-white sand
a bedroom where I sleep and wake
a sense of peace in safe places
until they fade to grey despair

it's too clean here to be a cell
no cockroaches or rats or dust
no tin cups rattled across bars
no inmates' anger down long halls
silence displaces every sound
yet a cell it is and I am here

set in the prairie outside town
our church stands in new snowfall
winter postcard of bygone days
bells on Sunday ring out worship
we go down to a basement room
upstairs grownups sing the hymns

fearing to sleep I lie in prayer
hope each night the man won't come
where is God in the dark of night
while I wait the nightly visitor
a shadow in a room with no light
it's no god who comes to my bed

dressed all in black like a crow
I stand at the edge of the dance
talk with some boys and drink shots
watch girls dance with each other
music fades as mist erases dancers
crow left alone in a concrete box

this island is sacred they tell me
spirit home where many dead live
near dusk the wooded path changes
mist drifts across from the marsh
spirits come to welcome me home
ahead on the path a crow waits

these days darkness sets in early
the silence of the crow lingers
shadows come alive in the corners
dance to the rhythm of marching feet
lines scratched into concrete walls
count the days between then and now

through eyes closed against the light
sunshine from the window blinds me
stuck in a corner of this white room
heavenly voices around me shine
so sweet in words I can't understand
long to go back to my simple cell

unable to make the slightest move
this tired body no longer my home
my travels out of body out of time
tallied on a wall somewhere safe
where I want to be floating free
far from this empty eternity

angels in white hold me prisoner
with needles and numbing potions
lock me inside this dead body
as gentle mist rises around me
far away I hear Julia calling
come to me my darling come to me

the custodians of this white room
come near and talk about my state
as though I neither hear nor see
while I travel between far worlds
no longer tied to time's passing
as the room fades and disappears

there are no walls only the mist
Julia takes my hand as we walk
unclothed as seraphs to our bed
our hearts ease as we lie close
at last I am where I need to be
soft she whispers I do love you

to softly touch

autumnlike before our springdance
leaves whisper soft to the ground

whitelimbs bare dancing the snow
fallenlife 'til wintering

we in duskyroom dancing
pause a moment to softly touch

this love

sometimes,
you just don't fall in love
like some fortunate accident

you turn your head slightly
see love at your side
as though it's been there
all along each day of your life
perhaps much longer than that

this love is familiar and comforting
an old friend you've known
for all eternity and you know
this love has been with you always
know this love will be with you
throughout all time

this is something other
not fallen nor in-love either
this love and you are
just that two become one
for all time past and future
and for the present especially

Turning

You never know just where the world will go
When you're turning,
When you're burning.
Turn, turn my head around again and dance,
Dance airy reels the sun reveals and lights,
and I'll dance too.

You never know just where the world may be
Or where I'll be
When you're turning.
We were together when the sky was young–
Remember when we were together, Love–
Now you're dancing.

Bend, never turn toward yes this, my world
In your burning,
Ever turning.
You never know just where the world will go,
In airy reels that light reveals at nights,
When you're turning.

Summer Somewhere

I've dreamed of a summer somewhere
Where the sun is always high,
Shining through the clear air
Above both you and I.

I seek all starlight,
I seek the sun–
Oh summer somewhere,
You are the one.

As you walk out in the meadow,
Go to brook and go to sea,
Sailing as the birds go
Sailing, sailing free.

And I watch you in the forest,
Best of woman, best of light,
Flower that gives no rest
Shining in the night.

Oh summer somewhere,
Oh where are you–
Sing me your lovesong,
None less will do.

I've dreamed of a summer somewhere
Where the sun is always high,
Shining through the clear air
Around both you and I.

she jumps me

she jumps me, she jives me, she drives me
passes by me, deep soul kisses me, sucks
my heart up out of my mouth deep into her

we talk across a table and beer, and my soul—
I see my soul shine somewhere in her eyes
I see and know as she is now mine I am hers

we are as naked in this public place as later
we will be undressed, the taste of each other
like sacred manna feeding our now united souls

naked words pass between us, our eyes hearing
bare truths as they pass between us, our eyes
locked on naked words, our shared souls passing

between us eternity opens up and momentarily
we are one within eternity and know we share
not some eternal truth at all, but each other

portrait

when she's done cooking and simmering pots
paint the kitchen air with frail wisps of steam
mystical in their dreamlike soft focus
she leans forward out across the counter
her hands pressing down on the counter top
her heels raising her off the kitchen floor
as she gazes out the kitchen window
at some distant dream or nearer drama
as some rhythm in her swings her hips
softly as though anticipating me
standing erect in the doorway watching

eden

in the garden waltzing beneath the apple tree
you and I naked as Adam and Eve
dance the spring and summer away in innocence
fail to see the sunshine turn to dusk
wrapping our waltz in the yard's darkening cloak
as we turn and turn and turn again
revolve and evolve until we are something else
waiting to be born in the coming darkness

garden party

at first there were no strawberries
only man and woman naked and God
wrapped in regal strawberry robes
the man on the grass watching
God touch her wrist seductively

strawberries are important here
held and hugged and lain upon
surrogates for love's embrace
sex toys and hats and statues
metaphor among the naked mass

everywhere in the park the naked
abandon decorum with lust for sex
games played without love or joy
while in the pool the naked women
gasp as men and beasts circle round

where the city burns in darkness
no strawberries or naked passion
suffer souls to pain without end
where on every corner danger lurks
and the garden party is no delight

footsteps in the garden

when birds go silent,
chipmunks and squirrels
rush to the underbrush,
the wind whispers soft
then goes dead quiet
leaving only a vacuum

I can feel them come,
the silent footsteps
along the forest path
echoing my own steps
until I stop and turn
and there is nobody

on the path behind me
there is nobody at all
but somewhere back there
a single tree rustles
though there is no wind
and I walk more quickly

hurriedly walking home
I can feel someone follow
though when I turn to see
there is only the rustle
only the empty wooded path
until I turn to walk again

at home I lock the gate,
cross the garden quickly,
go in and lock the door,
breathe a sigh of relief–
but in the silence I hear
footsteps in the garden

this acoustic world

there's a hush you hear
if you'll just listen
the song of the trees
whispers in the air
settled like morning
mist above the path
rising with the breeze

I talk to the trees
but they don't listen
says an old love song
yet stop on the path
listen to the trees
follow their voices
to another world

what is it you hear
along woodland paths
perhaps leaves rustling
the wind's melody
harmonies of trees
if you stop to hear
to listen to trees

the dance

there is more to the dance than just music
there is more than crowded floors and bright lights
there is a union beyond our bodies
an intimacy in the dancer's mind

in my fantasy I am one with you
as we dance across a blue starlit sky
embraced by the moon and by each other
painting swirls across the sky with our love

we are dancers, you and I are dancers
in some magical sky where our hearts join
and we are free of all but each other
where all that matters is us and our love

I would photograph you

I would photograph you in just that way
you reclining among the windblown grain
the sun winnowing its light through your hair
your cotton summer dress soft in its light

you would be resting there in the sunlight
gazing up the hill at that warm farm home
inviting you to come when you're ready
like that shining city you see in dreams

I would add colour to this photograph
clover perhaps or daisies in the breeze
and bright paint on that old grey house and barn
and add a bright print to your cotton dress

I would photograph you in just that way
lit by sunlight in a world of flowers
where songbirds sing and the sun seeks you out
but, most of all, I would photograph you

evening rain

I would sit with you on a park bench
early evening rain whispering to us
sheltered under just one umbrella
loving each other without saying

I would hold you close in the rain
loving you quietly and completely
as though this bench were all time
and all eternity were ours to share

I would love you in the rain as always
I have loved you in sunshine or shadows
my heart and soul become yours alone
you and I forever together in the rain

clouds

you and I were friends once
singing wide eyed love songs
loving two for oneness
you and I in our dance.

clouds were painted fluffball
lion's manes in breezes
drifting parachutists
breaking up old friendships.

rain today recalls you
storm so long ago now;
where are your eyes, Love, wide
as the clouds are melting?

Rain

Walking out in the rain one day,
I met a friend of mine
And we walked our road together a way
And said we both felt fine.

Well the time came that we must part,
My dear dear friend and I–
As gifts, I gave friendship and she her heart
Baked in an old style pie.

Who are you dreaming of...?
Is it a small child far away
Crying for her mother?
Is it an old woman of another day
Crying for your love?

(It screams with all the latent fury
of the hatred that lies
in love.)

Carelessly I ate the humble heart pie -
Digested, divested
Part of a friend; part of a lie;
Part love proved and tested.

Who are you dreaming of...?
Are you dreaming a brand new life,
The kind you wish you had?
And how real is your dream, or life
Crying out for love?

(It screams with all the latent fury
of the hatred that lies
in love.)

Walking out in the rain one day,
I met a friend of mine
And we walked along together a way
And said we both felt fine.

The problem is my thoughts are all locked up inside
Peering from a private little cage where they hide...

(sanity is a strange thing.
you lose it so easily
when you're tired
when you're drunk
when you're angry
when you've lost
a friend
an enemy
a lover
hope.)

A mind is a large empty room
In which two persons meet.

Who are you dreaming of...?
Is it a small child far away?
Is it an old woman of another day?
Are you dreaming a brand new life,
And how real is your dream, or life
When there is no love?

(It screams with all the latent fury
of the hatred that lies
in love.)

Walking out in the rain one day,
My dear dear friend and I–
Part of a friend and part a lie
That said we both felt fine.

Who are you dreaming of...
Crying for her mother,
Crying for your love,
The kind you wish you had;
Crying out for love?

(Part a friend and part of me,
it screams with all the latent fury
of hatred that lies.)

upstairs the dogs howl

the anger wails breathless words at her
fast as slam poetry or dark rap
beat-boxing and pounding her soul

her anger echoes through the black riff
resounding across the space between
widening cracks where once had been love

this raw call and response will not end
echoes across the void between them
while the dogs howl a dark harmony

and I will dance

in her place upstairs her music is playing
her music is playing with a solid beat
like her heart reaching out in mid-afternoon
not loud but felt in the apartment below

her music is playing with a solid beat
her pumping heart only just heard through the floor
through the ceiling of the apartment below
where another sits and finds fault with the world

her music is playing with a solid beat
her heartbeat spreading softly out the window
her heartbeat fading across the neighbour's lawns
to pause where the children play in the sunshine

from the place downstairs anger cries out loudly
against the beat against the beat of her heart
against the world in unfair rage against her
unfair and angry and she will take no more

her heart is pumping the words she cries out loud
I will bring over the neighbourhood children
I will bring over all the neighbour children
and I will dance
        and I will dance
                and I will

Flight Risk

Her soaring thoughts bear her up on gossamer and
hard realities, her wings carry me with her
to another place only her mind can take mine
and with her I soar upward as I've never soared.

*"I am a flight risk teetering on some slight edge,
ready to flee at a moment's notice,"* she says.

There is a small brown bird, a finch, unpresuming,
tourists buy in cages from asian street sellers
because her singing is so sweet, so beautiful
and, before the tourist reaches home, the bird dies.

What cage shall I build and of what material
will not forever stop her soaring singing heart?
How clip those wings of fantasy and hold her in
never again to soar so high and I soar too?

What risk in flight is so great it must be taken
away and the blue sky blocked from view and the wings
never again to soar nor that brown bird's sweet song heard,
its heart stopped at the bottom of some bamboo cage?

She is a flight risk, no doubt, but that's the tension,
the beauty of her as something in her flies high
escaping to some realm all her own and sometimes,
just sometimes carrying me with her to rapture.

I would take the risk to fly away in her wake
and if she turned away and flew beyond my reach
would still have known the joy of glorious flight
while somewhere in the wild a small brown bird still sings.

*"I am a flight risk teetering on some slight edge,
ready to flee at a moment's notice,"* she says.

The Uncaged Bird

It's letting her go that's most difficult
releasing her and knowing she'll fly home
but knowing sometimes pigeons don't return
knowing that she's free to fly her own course

It's letting her go that's most difficult
releasing the hawk from your wrist to fly
into some unknown sky and distant heart
land she may decide to make her new home

It's letting her go that's most difficult
freeing this songbird from her bamboo cage
to fly perhaps to yet another cage
or else to sing for all the world to hear

It's letting her go that's most difficult
never placing her in a cage at all
watching as she flies off to somewhere else
never knowing if she'll come back to me

some times of night

Some times of night the world seems far away
So like a life we dream to have some day,
While all around the mists obscure and hide
The world of man from man who would reside,
A spiral snail aloof among the dew
Of high rise grass and wait the reaper's shoe
That ends the day to leave behind crushed shell,
'Though where the snail has gone no one can tell.

And yet does not this snail become the mist
About a dream another world has kissed
With love and made by love to be its own
So that again the sower's seed is sown,
This time no reaper waiting to receive
Nor shell aspiral needed to deceive.

Because You Were

Thirty three is not a pretty time to die:
Just as the desert starts to green again
And just before those wild red flowers bloom;
Not yet quite half-way from the beginning
And certainly–God! Certainly not the end!

Because you were my friend; because you were.

I believe I've seen some of the handwriting
Scrawled hopelessly across your walls in red;
I believe I've done some writing myself,
Left my name in rainwater on your mind
In the hope it would not evaporate soon.

Because you were my friend; because you were.

Oh no, thirty three is not a pretty time,
But you'd struck a match or two in darkness
As seeds for gardens of wild red flowers.
(What great torches had you planned to plant there
And what vast deserts cultivate with green?)

Because you were; because you were my friend.

Yes, I believe I have been in your garden,
And while I don't know what you've planted,
If you read the handwriting on my walls
You'll know now of my obligation
To plant for you some wild red flowers. Flowers,

Because you were my friend.

Hands

You opened the door
And lit lamps with your eyes
What fire your eyes could rear
And your hands like a gardener
Planting a rose
Wandered over me, pleasing me
Rearing wild rose
And I built up my house with your mind.

When we closed the door
And we lowered the lights
In dusk our eyes would meet
And your hands like a gardener
Raising the flame
Wandered over me, making me
Wildflower tame
And you ate with the host of my mind.

Now I've closed the door
And I've shut off the lights
But still your eyes are here
And your hands like a gardener
Plucking a rose
Wander over me, teasing me
Lighting old glows
'Though I've emptied the house of your mind.

And your hands like a gardener
Casting a seed
Wandered over me, pleasing me
Lighting the rose
But I've weeded the house of your mind.

street of dreams

a street painted in darker shades
blues and blacks just beyond sundown
lamp posts supporting cones of light
staged yellow circles in the dark
fading to the vanishing point

now two figures enter stage right
pause in a spotlight as they swing
silhouettes who dance in the dark
slow waltz to some private music
drums brushed under bass and soft sax

dancing through the circle of light
for the moment young lovers pause
swirl softly between blue shadows
swing silhouettes in the spotlight
dance to the jazz in the night air

dance to the blue sax in the dark
swing and sway to the next lamp post
waltz on to the next and the next
twirl in the painted circle of light
on an uncertain street of dreams

where the street becomes indigo
shadows and lamplight fade and die
somewhere past the vanishing point
a lone sax whispers in the night
this jazz waltz only lovers hear

sympathetic resonance

the walls between us in truth
are no thicker than sorcery,
ephemeral screens revealing

all that ever has been
all that ever shall be
all the demons set free

in the corner
an old piano
waits to be played

the dancers are tableaux
dancing still in this dark
uncertain place and time

in this ballroom it is 1923
phasing through mists to 2021
redolent of ancient jazz

in the silence
an old piano
waits to be played

dark ancient fears reborn
dance ephemeral as jazz
frozen in and outside time

shadow dancers in the dark
terrors at a ball in 2021
dreams of dancers in 1923

hid in shadow
a man in a tux
patiently waits

slow motion and soft focus
an old song's echo in the air
tableau dancers come to life

dance to drive the fear away
dance oh dance brave souls
yet still shadows dance too

the shadow man
at the piano
a haunting tune

fifties café poetry reading

tabletop linoleum
accepts my elbow
and submits as though
I were an old friend
it had known long ago

the wooden chair wracks
my knees with history
while they grow numb
from sitting here too long and
jukebox jazz becomes cold noise

up front a poet reads banal jokes
with pregnant pauses and porn
suggests some bedside cosmic
witchcraft exists for the lovers
like a universal law of love

I press my elbows deeper
cherish the comfort of old lino
imagine squares with cameras
let my thoughts blur into grey
far from this curtain of poems

read aloud

the words don't matter
here only
caress wash ravage rush
through and across
senses of sound
writ everywhere

it is not written
it is not
                written
it is
        not written

the moving finger
writes but having
writ leaves
cold stone remains

take two
and call me
he said
                not wrote
call me
                not write

right
the power is
not in but
behind and before
the words

in the beginning
perhaps
but thought
sound and light
energy pure
and simple
electric power
also
were and were
with

the first and all
saying by
eye gesture intonation
flow flux howl rant rave
dance fire smoke captive
words undone
doing

here
the power is
only
  the words
don't matter

meeting

there are poems
outside
what I write

poets beside me
burning bushes
they made themselves

why choose one
smile for the cat's
jive is more hep

blowing crazy lines
Cheshire and glib
ivories glinting dark

between webbed branches
crimson lip
synchs that flick open

mouthed words like cats
have teeth and they
glisten pearly white

in the shower
bloody makeup runs
singing in the rain

not words but scat
the safe refrain
from unknown forms

words don't do do
they at times like
this outside time

you face lips suspended
bleeding in the rain
burning in the bush

the girl

the voices are there hidden in the night
where the girl can hear their every word
hidden behind corners and whispering
secrets along the street and in the trees

she shivers in the darkness and moves on
knowing the shadows follow and whisper
not only secrets but darker threats
all in languages only she understands

somewhere near an owl's hollow hoot calls her
her name echoes off the city's hard walls
cats' wails follow in a bitter harmony
the girl only half understands but fears

the street falls silent but the girl hears still
shadows whispering darkly toward her
the hush following her every step
she falling into ever deeper dark

sometimes the girl hears footsteps behind her
she turns to look but sees only the darkness
she sees the shadows slide along the walls
she shivers in the darkness and moves on

there is no sky behind the ink of night
the moon hides behind a black mask of clouds
someone has broken the streetlight bulbs
the voices are there hidden in the night

she shivers in the darkness and moves on
shadows move slowly along the dark walls
shadows whisper dark threats only she hears
she shivers and moves on through the darkness

somewhere far away a siren shrieks out
the siren bounces lightly off the walls
The girl hears only voices that follow
she hears only the whispers in the dark

a far away siren meets the darkness
the wail underscores a jazz song
owl and cat harmonize with the siren
the girl hears but only half understands

the girl is alone in the darkest night
a darkest night hides deep inside the girl
there is no escape from the voices' whispers
there is no escape from the creeping dark

somewhere near an owl's hollow hoot calls her
an owl in the city how strange she thinks
her name bounces off hard walls into black
cat's wails follow her name into the dark

the girl hears voices no other can hear
she hears and she understands dark whispers
threats in the night touch the girl deep within
hide behind corners and whisper to her

the dark grows thicker to smother the girl
not ink now the dark becomes living tar
the girl is wrapped in a black tar blanket
from somewhere the girl hears a siren call

the voices are there hidden in the night
she shivers in the darkness and moves on
somewhere near she hears an owl's hollow call
the street falls silent but the girl hears still

sometimes the girl hears footsteps behind her
she shivers in the darkness and moves on
there is no sky behind the ink of night
somewhere far away a siren calls her

night's dark blanket scares her only a while
deep in her heart she feels new warmth growing
she drowns in night's warm comforting embrace
falling into deep sleep the siren wakes her

fear releases the girl and blankets the warmth
in her heart is only the darkness she fears
in the night there is nobody to save her
there is only the shadows and the song

a scream slices the dark startling the girl
a scream seems to come from her own body
nobody hears nobody hears but her
she turns toward the darkness and moves on

somewhere in the night a jazz song plays
dark harmonies draw her into darkness
the dark rhythm carries past some threshhold
carries the girl toward dark beyond night

the voices are there hidden in the night
where the girl can hear their every word
and shivers in the darkness and moves on
and knows the shadows follow and whisper

shadows whisper from deep in dark corners
secrets told on the street and in the trees
not only secrets but darker threats
told in languages only she understands

the girl is alone in the dark crying
nobody hears nobody knows but her
the girl follows a sound through the darkness
from somewhere she hears a jazz melody

dark voices whisper to her through the night
threats in the night touch the girl deep within
somewhere far away a siren shrieks out
somewhere near she feels something dark approach

she sees only shadows hears only the song
nobody hears nobody knows but her
She shivers in the darkness and moves on
shadows follow slowly along dark walls

the girl hears voices no other can hear
she hears and she understands dark whispers
there is no escape from the whispered voices
there is no escape from the creeping dark

the jazz music draws the girl deeper
dark harmonies pull her toward darkness
the girl walks deeper into the darkness
there is no escape from the creeping dark

the voices are there hidden in the night
the girl hears but cannot escape them
hidden behind corners and whispering
secrets through the trees and along the street

the scream echoes louder in the darkness
there is no escape from the creeping dark
there is no escape from screams in the night
the girl has lost her way in the darkness

shadows move slowly along the dark walls
She shivers in the darkness and moves on
knows the shadows follow her and whisper
whisper dark threats that only she can hear

something in the night reaches deep in her
she shivers and walks into the darkness
she drowns in night's warm comforting embrace
the girl falls into perfect sleep to dream

the sun shines brightly from clear blue skies
threatening voices and dark shadows hide
the girl is at peace in a perfect day
far away a jazz song fills the air

shamus

gentle as light rain
the jazz blows soft
echoes blue and grey
shades of the street
awash in October dusk

hands in trenchcoat pockets
fedora tipped over eyes
wary of shadowed threats
I walk this street alone
slow as the saxman plays

look back and light up
in lamplit circle soft
as the rain is falling
become a shadow still
waiting for something

to happen in evening rain
alone under a streetlight
watched like I'm crazy
by a guy playing soft
jazz on an alto sax

jazz café

blowing sax
in shadow-stippled
dank basement
beatnik café
begets
black and white
images

cleo laine
sings soft
blues baby blues
as john
dankworth blows
cinematic jazz riffs
into the night

abandoned souls
finding refuge
among shadows
in the corner
whisper
blue moods
softly

the words lost
in reefer
smoke
poets read
cleo sings soft
dankworth wails
jazz soothes

recital

jazz fingers dance across the keys
in pas de deux and playful pirouettes
leap high in spinning dervish whirls
drop to hiphop backspin breakdance
street beats bop the blues become
kickdancing Cossacks flung airborne
arms outspread in joy drop to knees
slide glissando across white tiles
rise en pointe poetic music box slow
channel Chopin Gershwin Jerry Lee
rock steady beat goes on and on
and on the keys jazz fingers dance

this is for the jazz

under the African sun a lone man
quiet and lost in thoughts of home
nears his village and his family
hears drums breaking the silence
music and the voices of his people

for a thousand years and forever
the bright sun shines down on him
as he walks somewhere in Africa
music in the air calling him home
as the heart of his people sings

this postcard image never changes
could be any man anywhere in Africa
soon to return to his village
the music calling and the sun high
unaware of the dark coming soon

from village to sea a long walk
shackled and yoked two by two
across plains and through jungle
a lone man walks quiet and lost
in his heart he hears the drums

each man walks alone to the sea
one of hundreds from all Africa
in his heart his people's music
in his soul the soul of the land
in the dark his growing sorrow

this space is never really lit
boards creak and water seeps in
tightly packed families huddle
the few yams not enough to eat
silent sorrow where was music

the dead still take up space
stench of death everywhere
stench of shit and urine and
yams cannot stop starvation
slow death the only way out

one by one they step on deck
bright morning sunlight blinds
city noises deafen and terrify
hear the drums hear the music
hear memory held in the heart

some things cannot be enslaved
hearts in the fields sing Africa
hearts in the cities sing Africa
music freed from captive hearts
captures the music of America

In the silence of my life
I feel music all around
even in the hardest times
O I hear that joyous sound

I look back upon my life
see the changes ebb and flow
hear the music in the air
O the sound that I love so

on a wooded island
in the absence of owls
winds whisper ghost notes
sing through leaves at dusk
wash along the lake's shore
slip across the waiting water
seek distant horizons

new music grown from old roots
blossoms in café culture
the jazz café and juke joint
speakeasy and underground club
give birth to something new
welcome poets and songsters
jive talk and talking blues

the jazz age is born in America
overtakes Paris and the world
births dub and rap and hip hop
births beatniks and hippies
brings underground culture
beats songs chants of Africa
reborn heartbeat of us all

on night's rainswept city streets
impatient umbrellas sprout
passing cars swish like brushes
ride and snare catch the groove
winds around corners saxophonic
sounds of the city orchestrated
fragments of joy dance to the beat

In the silence of my life
I feel music all around
even in the hardest times
O I hear that joyous sound

I look back upon my life
see the changes ebb and flow
hear the music in the air
O the sound that I love so

stop for a moment and breathe
take a long slow breath
wait
don't breathe
it's in the air
can you feel it
can you hear it
it's all around you
breathe it in
breathe in deeply
breathe in the scent
taste it on your tongue
feel it fill your lungs
wait
breathe out and in again

can you feel it
it's all around you
it's in you
the heart of the sharecrop
the soul of street and tenement
the anthem of America
a whisper from chained masses

a lament for humanity
it's in you
can you feel the sorrow
can you taste the joy
a whisper become a cry
heard around the world

sung soft in slave quarters
sung sad on old wood verandas
sung along northern city streets
seen in a black and white world
photographs and field recordings
black men with battered guitars
black women and children in rags
not the blues but something else
songs of sorrow perhaps perhaps
songs of sex and life and love
songs to raise new hope and joy

In the silence of my life
I feel music all around
even in the hardest times
O I hear that joyous sound

I look back upon my life
see the changes ebb and flow
hear the music in the air
O the sound that I love so

this is for the jazz
this is for all the jazz
all the jazz filling the air
all the jazz bringing life
this is for all that jazz

this is for the sax
that drifts through the dusk
drifts though the dusk to evening
drifts from evening to absolute dark
this is for the dark that is jazz

this is for the minor keys
for the sad and sombre keys
keys that keep us awake at night
wistful keys and expectant keys
keys that bring us hope

this is for the keys that rock
boogie woogie keys in the night
keys behind that green door
wonder just what's going on
but this is just for the jazz

this is for slow groovy keys
piano bar keys for Domino keys
for Fats Waller piano roll jazz
for the cat in the local bar
and the artiste in Carnegie Hall

this is for the rhythm
bass and drum heartbeat
beat of factories working
beat of men and women
the beat the beat the beat

born of hope and sorrow
wrapped up in the blues
the heartbeat of Africa
syncopated with ragtime
reborn from dixieland
in creole street clubs
spread to every nation
jazz risen from slavery
beloved around the world

in slave ships from Africa
in southern fields of sorrow
in dark streets of tenements
in smoky cafés and speaks
fed by heartbreak and joy
touched by classical music
laced with folk and country

a culture nurtured by time
moist and alive and reaching
always growing yet the same
through time and distance
from small African villages
to America black and white
now spread all 'round the world

In the silence of my life
I feel music all around
even in the hardest times
O I hear that joyous sound

I look back upon my life
see the changes ebb and flow
hear the music in the air
O the sound that I love so

the woman

it begins with a room
pale red and cool blue light
scattered silhouettes at tables
soft saxotones wafting
through cigarette smoke
and casual conversation

at the bar a splash of light
seems meant to expose
the woman who waits
slowly sips her drink
waits for something
waits for someone
waits deep in a shadow
no light can erase

sorrow bends the woman
leans her forward
slumped with elbows
abject on the bar
slow sipping her drink

on the woman's right cheek
a tear draws a damp line
downward echoed by sax
lines cutting the smoke
underlining her blue mood
another tear slides
another tear and another

the woman knows nothing
will happen now at this bar
the woman knows nobody
will come to meet her here
the woman knows nobody
knows her sorrow
what she has lost

the music stops

the woman stands
a quick perhaps furtive
glance at near human
silhouettes in the smoke
walks slowly to the door
lets in the sunshine
only for a moment

there is only the sax
again caressing the air
and the sad silhouettes
under red and blue lights

the woman is gone

homecoming

as she walks down the endless street
the weight of years on her shoulders
the woman fades out of sight and mind
another tattered stranger invisible
among the shades living on the edges

doors will not open when she knocks
seeking food or a warm place to rest
or will open only to turn her away
she walks slowly as though in pain
weary bones they say but it's worse

overtaken by eternity the woman walks
deep in her heart a teenaged princess
asleep in a tower of memory and regret
rising dark and cold along the way
lined by the lost bundled in blankets

a young woman once danced and laughed
enjoyed the attention of handsome men
now fades into long ago and far away
dreams and shadows along the edges
an old woman walks ever more slowly

once there was a man she had loved
two boys and a girl grown and gone
good friends and successful career
magic lantern images flicker past
fading shades of once upon a time

the woman shivers by the closed door
no doorway offers safety or stops wind
tight-pulled coat offers little comfort
sleep fills with dreams of other lives
this street leads nowhere but the end

passersby don't deign to see sad eyes
rumpled humps at the sidewalk's edges
outstretched hands and empty paper cups
unwanted and unseen as nearby trash bags
this woman's world has come to this

in summer she rests on park benches
on grass under a tree near the shore
in cold neon-lit downtown corners
in winter she hugs herself tightly
without shelter warmth is an old coat

spring air and sunshine free and clear
the girl runs through her small village
far away and long ago yet here and now
an old woman sleeps on a city sidewalk
dreams comfort better than a coat does

in dreams she recalls worlds long past
was she that happy girl she remembers
could that smart-looking woman be her
days all the same have become years
the woman has lost count of all time

the woman walks along slowly now
tired not just of walking but of life
a ghost among ghosts on these streets
ahead a bus stop shines like a beacon
shelter against the cold night winds

bundles by her on a bus shelter bench
a weary woman not ancient as she looks
shivers sleeps dreams a life long ago
walks to sunlit green fields and lakes
childhood friends on village greens

the world is still wrapped in dark night
the woman wakes to the dawn's silence
sees light of a new day far ahead of her
opening in the dark at the street's end
the woman rises and walks into the light

*Al Capone may be remembered as a notorious gangster,
but he had other interests besides breaking the law. He
had a lifelong love of music. He strummed the tenor banjo
and mandola when he was in prison, learned to play a
number of songs, and even played in a band with other
inmates at Alcatraz.*

The Boston Globe, May 15, 2018

the soft side

Al's new crew was The Rock Islanders
no jailhouse rock this but show music
jazz and every popular style of song

talk about a multi-talented guy
tried to relieve the daily grind
playing banjo, guitar, and mandola
an instrument like a large mandolin

Al racked up time for good behaviour
took up music playing banjo in the band
and a rotating group of musicians
played with Al in the band as a privilege

first I learned a tenor guitar Al wrote
*then a tenor banjo and now the mandola
but for solo work only*

when it came to his many victims
thought to have died in gang wars
many at his own hand
Al was heartless

but when it came to his family
Al apparently had a soft spot

an intimate letter penned from prison
suggests this ruthless racketeer
handled tenderness almost
as skillfully as his Tommy gun

he even wrote a love song "Madonna Mia"
wrote his son saying *when I come home*
I will play that song and about 500 more
mostly theme songs from the best shows

in other words junior
there isn't a song written
that I can't play

when you get the blues sonny
put on one of the records
with songs I wrote you about

the obelisk

wheat stands gilt ready for harvest
each crown bent in anticipation

hand in hand we enter the field
wade through the golden waves
toward the grove at the centre
a leisurely flow like choreography
across the calm and quiet space
our accompaniment not strings
lark and oriole and whippoorwill

this is slow motion
like the clouds across the sky
like the hawk lazing a circle at the centre

a day out of time
a day to leave one's self behind
commune with some universal spirit

we are like that here
                    out of time
                                out of place

the chiaroscuro of the wood
dapple of light among the black
makes all reality appear unreal
puts the lie to any notions
we might have had of noon

the feel is not of ghouls and grasping shadows

we enjoy our walk across the dampness
fallen leaves with the untimely shade
the soft breeze cooling us

what dark shadows might threaten
the slender darts of the sun melt
or soften to nothing more dangerous
than the sodden leaves underfoot

after the webbed shadow of the trees
the sun seems brighter than before
we pause at the edge of the grove
uncertain of our eyes

the field here is almost exactly
as the one we have left behind us
grain as gold
sky as blue
clouds as brightly glowing

except in the distance there is a shadow
perhaps of coming rain
and the hawk is nowhere to be seen
none of this surprises me

what does is the obelisk

it stands in the middle of the field
white and redolent of sunlight
possibly twenty metres tall
at its top
the life size figure of a man
his stance and attitude of attention
feet together
hands at his sides
face forward and upward

caught in some undertow of flowing grain
we gravitate from the shadows
toward this misplaced monument

as we move toward him
the man on the pedestal slowly raises his arms
outward
sideways
to shoulder height

we are almost at the base of his tower
the man falls forward into nothingness

my heart stops
every function of my body stops
I feel the hand I hold in mine
convulse and tighten

the man sails gracefully forward
downward then upward
a broad spiral ever narrowing
toward the sun.

her grip on me loosens
life returns to my body

this man sails like a bird
ever upward until
I can barely see his form

he is shrunk to the size of a distant sparrow
still he moves
toward the burning centre of the sky
I watch his form gyre against
the soft white of the clouds

his is not the only dark form I see

above him is the shadow
seen earlier in the distance
moving closer now
downward as he moves upward

only as it begins its dive do I see
in it the shadowy shape of the hawk
the hawk after that sparrow
that soaring, flying man

she touches my hand again

I turn to look at her
a young woman with raven hair
her eyes reflecting the drama
far above us

she is gripping me tightly

the sky melts away like plastic
everything is black

I am shaking
being shaken
her hand no longer grabs at mine
no longer pulls me back

I am floating free

the man was still rising
the shadow was still swooping
I do not know the ending

all I remember is that man
feet together and arms spread
like some Christ
suspended in the sunlight
that shadow dropping over him
onto him like some predator bird
and him not knowing

the Waldorf

here is an ageless dignity
which will not be denied

classic Alberta architecture
a mass of sandstone blocks
corniced and gargoyled
with sandstone sculpture
civilization and frontier daring

the Waldorf stands at the very beginnings
the corner of Railway Avenue and First Street
the site of the old Western Front Café
the beginnings of downtown Drumheller

at three storeys when built in 1921
tallest building in the entire district
five more storeys added six years later

a skyscraper

the Waldorf was bankrupt
by 1930 boarded up and left
derelict for nearly seven years
only the lower two floors opened
during the war years

Americans bought the hotel
in 1955 completely refurbished
restored the richness
that once had been

the Waldorf was reborn

we dine at the Waldorf
we walk into the past

the lobby is vast
opulent with hardwood
hazed by the patina of time

hardwood benches along wood panelled walls
interspersed by plants in massive oaken pots
and what must be the original brass spittoons

under the gaze of Sam Drumheller's portrait
the benches are graced with timeless men
holding newspapers and pipes or cigars
their decadence a matter of pride

we turn left
past the dark wood projection of the front desk
wait to be seated in the Badlands Restaurant
well-aged opulence the order of the day
brightened by tall, many-paned windows
white drapery and matching white tablecloths

it all looks very expensive.

dinner at the Waldorf done
once again we pass the massive hardwood desk
to the lounge at the lobby's opposite side

we settle comfortably into black leather
perhaps vinyl seats in our booth

wine at dinner and Grand Marnier after
ease conversation in this half-dark room

outside time or place
hardwood and vinyl floats us
beyond any known world

neutered rock and roll from the ceiling
erodes our conversation and our thoughts

we settle into the grey room with our drinks

among the hoodoos

sunlight flicks across
the hoodoos behind me

there is a feeling here
a power older than time
under a blue bowl of sky
that goes on forever

here is no past
         no present
         no future

A man on his own can feel
as the gods must feel

I am Prometheus rising
over one edge of earth
as the sun's light climbs
to meet me at the other edge

I stand at the edge of eternity
of knee level wild grass
facing the sun rising
from the primeval plain

I walk toward the ancient empty house
feel good here above the hoodoos
above the scrub and cacti
above all I've known worlds away

the house has stood a long time empty
paint gone with the prairie winds
most of the glass gone or cracked

the front door lolls open
seems to welcome me

I walk the distance slowly
enjoy the silence of dawn
the soft touch of the morning breeze

I climb the broken steps
cross the verandah
pause before going in

I ease the old door open
the top hinge broken
the bottom one creaking
pull outward
let the outside corner rest
on the verandah's wood floor

I step inside the entrance hall
the door at the end is closed

I pass the archway to the living room
the staircase leading upward
two doorways opposed
on the left and right sides
and open the door to the kitchen

the coal stove is still here
dust covered and spider webbed
traces of rust on the black
on the nickel trim

in another corner
a wooden table and one chair
its back broken

tattered curtains flank broken windows

the whole house is like that
traces of past life

chesterfields and mattresses ripped open
perhaps by mice making nests
by hunters turned vandal from boredom
in each room a piece or two of furniture
never a full complement

I pause in each room in turn
imagine the life this house has seen
imagine the owners as they were long ago

in my mind I repair the furniture I see
fill the rooms with what is missing
live for a few moments in each room

walking downstairs from the bedrooms
I feel the ancient bannister break away

justice

my messenger is not working well now
this devastating nonverbal beat heard
as though I see the world through a mirror
limited by an overnight raid somewhere
while a serpent come out of the north
wraps us around until it bites its own tail

this man looks at me with death on his face
and there is always a tongue in your mouth
but you don't make excuses for the man
cornered by dogs in a dead-end tunnel
while beneath the surface a fire glimmers
banked perhaps too long and turned to ash

hear us whisper
voices in the dust
hear our wailing
cries on the wind
hear our voices
waves on the water
hear us whisper
hear us hear us
as we rise again

under ashes of those who have come before
banked embers of the future wait their time
sleepers ready and waiting to light the way
justice is not patient nor always swift
no iron lady with torch and book in hand
no great colossus watchful at the shore

this is not anger seething beneath the dust
for below the ashes of all civilizations
Justice lies in wait as the dust settles
keeps a wary eye on the dark as it grows
waits the perfect moment to bring truth
and with truth, light again to the world

hear us whisper
voices in the dust
hear our wailing
cries on the wind
hear our voices
waves on the water
hear us whisper
hear us hear us
as we rise again

you imagine we've gone away long ago
the ancients and the ones who resist
the lost generation the beat generation
the hippie revolution and street warriors
people who stand up for love and justice
who cry out for peace and understanding

you think you can do things your way now
the resistance dead and buried long ago
in the ashes of a nation you set burning
in the ashes of a world you set burning
ashes meant to cover your dark history
ashes meant to bury resistance forever

listen as our voices rise from the ashes
lifted up in the renewed wind of change
hid too long beneath your smoke and ash
millions of voices raised in resistance
old guard and new generations in harmony
resonance of times past and times to come

hear us whisper
voices in the dust
hear our wailing
cries on the wind
hear our voices
waves on the water
hear us whisper
hear us hear us
as we rise again

dust devils in the wind we dance and spin
ourselves out of the ash bringing others
outliers you have not seen rise before time
out from the cracks between the movements
standing hand in hand in the spaces between
holding the line as we all move forward

cancelled or covered up by political noise
voices of protest and dissent rise together
rise from the ashes you laid so long ago
dust devils in the wind become the thunder
rise up to rain truth over the old drought
ashen upon the land and you fear the storm

hear us whisper
hear us hear us
as we rise again